Cocoa Blues

TAZ WEYSWEETE

1st edition ©Tasia Linton, Portsmouth, Va. 2015, Book Wook
2nd edition, Ceteris paribus , 2016, Wider Perspectives Publishing
ISBN: 978-1-537073-26-2
3rd edition, Ceteris paribus 2020 ISBN: 978-1952773-25-9

Table of Contents

You could never know how much it means to me that my words are on page. Thank you for believing in me when I didn 't.

For Mommy and Peaches

U said I would. Be damned. Xoxox

My Birthstone is Sapphire

Push

And the next thing you know, life is being pulled from your body. And u feel this shit. The legs, the arms, the head, the blood the cord. They are alive because of you. You did this. You did this. You did it.

Pull in

Wondering about God don't make you a believer.

Believing in God don't mean U won't wonder.

Pop

He got shot. U ever watch life leave the body when you know the feeling of bearing life from your own? Let me be clear, you die, too.

I believe in souls.
Souls cry too.
Bodies wear wounds and have health insurance.
Souls do not.

Exhale

I said to a friend yesterday, pain is pain... we are in it together but want to heal separately? What the fuck is that?

Jewel. The truth is the truth. The division is the proof that that won't matter. The soul deals in scales. Balance is key. So some shit will be right for you + other shit right for me. Some body is wrong.
Did U get that?

Now
Whether or not you did, it's still fact. And ain't that the bullshit?

Whether you get it or not
Life won't wait for you to catch up.
Your spirit might get there before your body does.

Stop.

It's only 9:25 a.m. on a Sunday.

I woke up like this.

BURST

The world will open up and burst its true colors like a paint gun pointed toward the heart. The color red will stand for love and symbolize pain. It will stain the lips and leave its trace on his face when we kiss. It will be the color of a sidewalk forever. Tucked inside the projects. They will walk past, but never forget when the blood pooled under him. They will never forget him falling to his knees. One mic dropped. Heineken bottles shatter. A shot that boomed too far past 9. Baby stops jumping on the bed. Gunfire raps at the door.

I pick up my daughters. The baby just turned 2. My big girl is 3. Take them to his mistress. Don t know this is her position then. We are both crying. He is lying on the ground. Tells me to back up. Eyes so big. Baby don t give up I can fix this. I call his mom. Mine isn t here. She s in Heaven. Cant leave a message. Heart is beating reckless. Desperate to call her awake before he falls asleep.

Fuck this shit. Call my daddy. He tears thru the streets, gets up in the EMTs face, put him in the ambulance its my son! Cause in the hood u gotta tell em first his address, + whats his name, this the projects he aint on the lease his kids live here. We live here! The streets get deep. So much blood. Tell his mistress thank you. I gotta go to the hospital. His mom is here now. Who woke her up? Im glad she s up. They say he is dying. I am crying I can t do it without him. Nurse says to calm me, we, his family + me are holding hands and praying. Doctors are crying. My daddy calls, he has my daughters, the oldest is awake now she asks, –My daddy got shot† My dad can't reason asking her if she knows what that means. At 3 she does. And he hugs her and tells her yes.

He lives.

7 lives later, he is in a coma. He is hooked to tubes in his nostrils. One lung ruptured, kidney gone, liver spliced. Lucky to be alive. Hair matted. He don t know me. I hold him. He don t hold me. This is ICU. His mom wants me to leave. I don t concede yet. Pictures of her and I on my back. Him and his daughters on my chest.

Wet eyes open. I am drunk in the emotional + physical. Like ritual I circle the hospital.

I haven t taken a shower in 3 days. He isn t awake. His mom makes it clear whos in charge. Who s the boss. His grandma has the girls, his aunt is helping. I have to work. Insides melting. 3 hours from job to him on bus, skin is melting.

This isn't a question of Love, naw cause know that I Loved him.   This isn't a question of us, cause loyalty will numb you and subconsciously overrun U into a forgiveness U don t mean. And I could talk about all of the surgeries, the worrying and the guilt. I could talk about the truths that silence will bring about. And I doubt you would believe all of the material things that I have lost, let alone time, youth, + family. Or that I tried to smoke + snort + drink + fuck away the pain.   Or even that he didn't deserve this. Or that leaving wasn't worth it. Or that beatings I took didn t make me feel any stronger. I thought worth less.

I could have never imagined that the sound of an intercom or jail cell would make me cringe

or that my babies voices or a kite
could ever make me cry

had thoughts like I don't believe in suicide but I ain't afraid to die.

that I would describe myself as a gargoyle as opposed to an angel.

Or that he would become a Devil,

in the reflection of God's bullseye.

Acceptance Poem

There will be no parade.
No band. No saints.
No song and dance.
No smiles. No hugs.
No recognition.
There will be no parade.
The air will be still.
Breathe deeply.
Wipe your tears.
Lift your chin.
There will always be work to be done.

Freewrites

If I had to say it plain, I could. U do not have to bind me by my wrists or sit me down. I m good. Silence is a gift to the wise. Not disguising opinion but the notion that my quiet makes my feelings known. This is presence this is acceptance. True temptresses don t attempt shit they make moves we do not fight for any side but teams choose. U lose if u ain t on mine. U know ain t nobody fuckin wit it. The only thing sugary sweet is word to my government. This covenant, these poems, my verbal agreement you have my word in lead ink and blood in love drink up a cup of this displace your suffrage vote for me walk in light or vex till you become golden then you ll b free off key rightness might just make the truth unbearable check the variables what is your hypothesis cause it seems to me you just knocking shit that don t love you back. Is this about understanding? Cause its not supposed to be this cracked. Language is futile. Make the word your missile detonator, I penetrate the outer lining of ya feelings leave you squirming I b beaming tis the season..... We b looking out for miracles we need some revelations Tryna write my story it b taking all my patience constant allegory Maury story TV stations got bitches fucking in the shower screamin yo we made it! Tired of the shuck n jive the 9 to 5 the matrix just wanna dream n smoke and write and hang out wit my

babies love up on my man learn all I can and b creative sit down with all the Homeys and play catch up on the basics the basis of this rhyme is to shine bring smiles to faces spit it from my heart never giving up aint no fake shit they b like is you rhyming? never stopped, Just killin stages... I always got a line or two to fill up any spaces.
Never been complacent never been Jamaican.
Guyanese till the death of me n I got it cause I make it. I'm exotic and I'm flagrant lil ratchet and amazing something like a stunner pick ya pen up fix ya faces...

Dating in Your 30s

Sometimes i wonder did my mother ever slip her arm underneath her lover's neck and kiss his nose and i suppose get to the business of making me or was i a drunk night where endorphins and explosions become the same thing and wedding rings are as cliche as cracker jack boxes and the prizes that were never of any value

757's Billie Holliday

They call me Billie.
Poet who spits the blues.
I choose to mimic this title with pride.

Boastful when sharing pain like some matriarch for
baby mama's and single women in their 30s, for
broken girls and poor kids and the overworked.

Now if I was to say that I understand life I'd be bold
face lying but there is no denying that I know pain.
I can't claim any happiness from understanding what
hurts people.
I do not find joy in making you cry
It is not my intention to make you remember and
become angry all over again
My poems are not for you
They are about me
Keeping me alive
I am in pain and writing helps me to not suffer the
suffocation I feel when breathing
Spitting on stage frees me,
like a panther coming to

feast
A beasts home. Lift my voice
into the sky
Break the air

Pinch the nothing between my fingertips till they snap
Keep snapping
Start humming too
Feel the tune brewing in my tummy leave my lips
Begin to kiss the sky

Soul came out in voice
Heartbeat pulses thru my hips
Flows from my legs to the top of my head
Waters return to balance in the original form
Swimming swiftly
Swaying deeply
Spitting frees me This is flying
I'm alive cause I keep writing. . .

The revolution will not b quiet

I.

I'm alive like a newborn's tears. Awake like information.
Endless like stars. Resilient like moon.   Inertia like
clouds. Broken like ripples + reflective like mirrors.
Questionable like, Red Pill. Blue Pill. Exhilarating like
shiver. Breathtaking like now. Gone But Present like
Dust. Original like world. Me, like no other

II.

So when I discover 2 esquires eating pork bellies +
sipping prohibition after bar.   The one lawmaker says
to the other, –they are waiting on a revolution that isn't
coming, a revolt that wont happen and a reaction that
they can rate.†

Don't u taste the deceit in the air.   Adding to the
deficit + throwing salt on these like people for snails,
receding into shells, heads nodding mouth nailed shut.
I tell them U gonna shrivel up and die before U catch
up + rise. Small fries muster to be busted by muskets.
Their blood disguised as rhetoric.

Hell, the government is heaven sent! The dollar makes
show of the pyramids! luedorem King of Nazareth:
–Constituents! I mean friends! We need U! Bear your
arms!   We share the same veins! Bulging like roots
under skin!   The blood of our constitution held within!
Built to carry flags! Made to salute! And work this great
land of America!†

Shit made me laugh.

I tapped lawmaker number one on his shoulder. Lawmaker number 2 turned around. I say to them both, my arms bare love, ancestry + legacy. Im an American poet. Got a minute for a constituent, I mean friend? I wanna spit something to U

III.

The revolution will not be quiet. It will not be hidden in words left on paper tucked away inside the pages of notebooks we don t open hoping to hold our dreams to ourselves or left on shelves to collect dust. The revolution will not be a prologue or a last page or play victim to coffee + grease stains or faded letters from blue + black ink that has spread on yellowing loose leaf from the heat of the sun s rays. It will not be marked thru. It will not be balled up. It will not be limited to characters. The revolution will not be quiet. The revolution will not be your girl or your old lady. Will not be addressed as an infant child or treated senile because of age. The revolution will not address you as the father it never had. The revolution wont use you daddy you can keep that. The revolution will not be quiet. The revolution will not be sexy, It just is. The revolution needs love. Love is that big. The revolution will not use its lips for your fantasy. Or be confined to the pixels in profile pics to be scratched

+ sniffed + dreamt about. Slept on. The revolution will be more than a face in a frame. The revolution will not be high. The revolution will not obey no swine! The revolution cannot be quiet. The revolution will eat at work so the revolution can afford to get into the venue. The revolution will miss her children to pay her dues. It will be loved correctly the revolution is done accepting anything less. The revolution will give U its best. The revolution will give U its all. This Black Girl Host Stands Tall. The revolution will cry itself to sleep. The revolution will stand on feet that hurt. The revolution will wear old clothes carry a boxcutter + ride with a bus pass. The revolution will not be quiet. So the revolution will update its facebook status + tweet. The revolution will write until its eyes blur from its phone screen. The revolution will be scared but fake brave every time onstage. She wont be quiet. This voice alone is gonna start a riot! So the revolution will be televised. Will be facebooked, will be emailed to as many as it can reach to as many as it can teach. To however many will listen without pretense. The revolution will have no intermission. The revolution is trained to go. The revolution don't believe in snitching, however it does believe in letting go. But not without speaking, so.

LIKE I SAID

I tapped lawmaker number one on his shoulder. Lawmaker number 2 turned around. I say to them both, my arms bare love, ancestry + legacy. I'm an American poet. Got a minute for a constituent, I mean friend? I wanna spit something to U

Food Stamps and Wine

Landlocked in a space where nothing grows but
distaste for the conditions.
The oppressed, not really? Guilty only of being
impoverished without enough knowledge to
know why. Don't spend yo food stamps on no
bread and buy wine!
The Pharisees don't know that they go together.
That this could b you paying tides, temple 711.
Chapter, I can t wait to get high, sigh. Sway.
Say mmmmm real hard and bite your tongue.
Hold the wrath of God behind your lips.
Kiss your fingertips, look them in the eyes and
say capiche
U understand.
Cause they don't do amen, to them, u are
Not really oppressed, u are afraid. Misguided,
no guidance, if u just try shit, u could change
your condition.
Take the criticism.
None of it matters,
we are labeled because everyone has the same insides,
from now on im only dealing with the generic and
store brands.
Sarcasm scanned.
Don't say i move your spirit when u don t care
to know from where it was inherited.
I once called my flow profuse cause I still want

to b Lauryn
Did her New Jeru get on the carpet in Babylon
Did his dreds hang like bars over her body
Like, lineage trumps privilege.
White privilege given polka dots.
She's still the poor kid at the bus stop.
He is still Marley.
Oppression.
Depression.
It is all the same.
A girl stood on stage at the Venue nd told us,
–there was no show, go home!†
And i thought, –it could all be so simple.†
(The pain, the pain. The pain)
Africa don't want me.   No matter how I throw
myself at it.
She is the best I never had.
Don't let them catch you buying wine.
They don't know that u just live and work nd
pray
They don't know it hurts sometimes
All of it
That maybe u couldn't move
Maybe u couldn't move
And all u know is that U don't like it here and
you weren't always broke or cheap
U didn't always need help

And u live and u work and u pray
U use your foodstamps to eat and the wine to
preoccupy your mind.

Another Ode (Queen Angel)

Dear Mommy,

Tonight, I really wish I could put my head on your thigh.
I cry when I'm happy, too. Nd I want to tell u that this
poet I saw on t.v. read my stuff and really liked it.
She emailed me and everything. I want to tell you this
young girl I admire is going to help me get published. I
want to tell you, I m going to b in an art show with my
paintings. My drawing on windowsills and walls was
never in vain. I want to tell you I m doing an interview
and photos for this dope website. I want to tell you that
I'm nervous about all of it. I want to tell you, I gotta try
to b what I told you I was gonna be. I want to tell you
how tired I really am. I want to tell you that I miss the
smell of your cooking. Sometimes I nail it, tho. I want
to tell you my kids ask about you. And I tell them how
dope you were. I want to ask you about my father. I
want to ask you about your mother. I want to tell you
that I get so lonely it hurts. I want to tell you why I had
to stop celebrating holidays.

I want to tell you how much evil I've seen.

I want to tell you how close I got to feeling loved.

I want to tell you that I love you.

I miss you.

Other people's mama's love on me, tho
I want to tell you that I've met some amazing people since you've been gone. They don't know how much I care. I am so awkward now.

I want to tell you so many things. But, really...I just wanna share a joint with my favorite girl and lie my head on your thigh till I fall asleep.

Love,
Masha Xoxox

A Love Poem to Myself, Reprised

This is a poem for the 420 pulitzer prize winner,
the vamp camp poet

Designing Drafts on stress + wishes. U battle
inner demons + last goodbyes. Holding true to the
belief that one day you will revolve around a sun
the way the Earth was meant to. U snap like U bend.

She who speaks emcee, U weeping willow of a woman.

U make people smile.

Echo laughter in hollow wombs. U quick with it + slick
talking. Find gladness in the ratchet + humor dry. Like
the world through your eyes. All bad decisions + good
intentions and one more times.

U begin again.
Take everything + nothing to heart.

U my favorite kind of hipster.

U 80s baby trapped in the 90s swag.

Thrift store tees + designer bags. Epitome of cool.
Naturalista. Still a Diva. U duffle bag lady

had too much stuff + missed her bus

smiling she thought of now, U miss one. Next, 15 ones coming.

U miss New York;

U miss New York

The Mason Dixon never opens her venus fly trap of a mouth. The bitch let Virginia eat U alive. But this is not a poem for where U have been or where U may never get back to. This is a poem for the tattoos etched into your skin + the stories they tell.

For the whirlwind on your neck + TMP.

For the praying hands that clasp a rosary.

For Diahann Denise.

For the wings between your shoulder blades + the dream catcher on your spine that reminds you that anything is possible when your head is bent.

This is not a poem for the men who never asked what
these stories meant.

Fuck the boys who have seen your stories so that U can
fuck the men who will read your fine print.

This is a poem for you. Some peace of mind.

Let it comfort U like

crying quiet tears, listening to poetry in the back of a
crowded room

over the last man U made love to.

He did not break U.

This is a poem for your hands. The henna markings of blue collar scars. For the length of your fingers + the shortness of your nails. For the weed + ash embedded beneath them. For the knuckles you pop constantly. For the protruding veins, from years of working and writing.

This is not a poem for the broken heart or worn spirit. This is a poem of acceptance. This is a poem for the mole on your butt. For the time your 3 month old daughter pulled down so hard on your earring that now you could wear gauges.

This poem is for that.

For how fly you is. Rocking bangles + old Timbs.

For the fact that U can rock a stage, a bus stop + your kid's school play with the same demeanor.

This is your poem. True friend poem. Do anything for your daughters + your son poem.

For the homey who cooks like they need a hug poem.

This is your love poem.

For the lack of tact and no regrets.

This poem is not a hype man.

This is not to rebuild the ego + go comatose from the accolades, Depending on if they like it or not, already you are so full of yourself.

This is a poem for standing when you felt like falling +
you were already down.
This is for the soul that wills the spirit to move
something. This is a poem for the days when U miss
everyone
+ being held is as foreign as forever and always.

When no one has told U in years, they can help U.

U have potential.

For U boo, standing on the cliff of supposition + now.
Laughter echoing from a womb barren + alive.

Barren but alive!

This is a poem for giving it your all no matter how little you had left to give.
For resonating a vibration that sustains U.
Maintains U.
This is for U boo. 420 scribe. Demon fighting.
Tactless. Sweetheart. U the 2nd coming of Wonder Woman,

Like when Nikki Giovanni penned +
they will never understand that all the while I was quite happy.

Dice

Shake.

Twist.

Grind. Pop seed.

2 fingers, maybe a thumb for fun.

Papers, vapors, capers! I gotta story to tell...

We laughed until we cried. Then cried until we laughed.

My babies kissed me! It felt good!

I believe.

I slept. Cooked. Reasoned.

Smiled at memories. Smiled at today.

Exhaled. Before and after Google.

Beautiful evolution.

Paperbag Poem

Indoctrination, Oedipus Complex, Willie Lynch. Don't flinch. Take that. Fall back into the definitions + realize that your definitions of relationships are seen thru different prisms in the eyes of the living depending on the extent of the heartbreak. Take that n listen. Love is speaking directly. While still finding itself immersed n wet dreams during the day. No more fucking that s around up or me. See. Ima mother but no mans mommy till my sons 18 + even than only if he becomes one. I am. A woman. No one s bitch. Can't get on all fours + satisfy no itch.

I need to be bathed. See I know their lies the man who will nurture my needs N I have been in a matter of words nurtured, already my heart is heavy I kinda need to talk about. Need a king. Who understands that he is one. Not walking behind me, letting me play the role of the mother I have become, because I am his woman. So he leads. He doesn't cheat + he would never cross the line because that could be detrimental to his legacy. No man would do that. Think thru that. Leave the trace of another races face on its family name.

Did U know U were beautiful. What a flower U could be if that seed was developed. If the amniotic fluid that enveloped U, was heaven water. And not a woman's misery. Or a mans revenge. Or their cry for help. Cause he wants to step up and she needs to fall back. They would know that their love was beautiful from the beginning that there is no ending + prosperity could be continuous if she could learn to kiss him + not see pain. And he didn't see superwoman broken as he holds her.

Y'ALL DONT HEAR ME DOE,

so just define the 1st 3 lines.

Take ya time wit it.

Who U?

I am not content with being surrounded by the unfamiliar. Your gentiles have no bearing here. I've seen yours and you ve seen mine. This is beyond crossing lines my dear, see I don't know you but U pressing me on some you the man shit on some hold your dick watch how you stand bitch every other word like a habit. Usually lying like you wipe your nose with paper made of sand. Shit.

This is unfamiliar. I'm uncomfortable. I don't know you. and I feel surrounded. Like by water. Yea I'm drowning. Sinking. Like your face into that flask or your body into that chair. And you say this is a conversation. My face reads devastation. Yours reads hurt. desperation. You wanna kno if U still got it. Warm and nasty newport breath and sour beer. Your kisses are rotten. Your soul tells on you in this moment. u couldn't b sweet if U tried. Back the fuck up. I told U. I'm uncomfortable with the unfamiliar. Mama said don't talk to strangers. I don't know. I suppose U would like us to remain friends make amends tell me to take one for the team like every day I don't take it for my seeds. Your eyes are yellow. They scare me. But you don't. I just see that there is truth inside of them. kinda trifling they don't do no confiding in your lips. And the left one just twitched. And u seem poised to flinch like demons have taking over your ears. I can only turn u away with a prayer furrowed in my eyebrows. I don't know you. And I'm uncomfortable with the unfamiliar.

Kings Play

She lets him inside.
Always letting him inside.
Allowing him to whitewash her walls as if she prefers that color to pink.
Allowing him to sink inside of her until she feels impaled.
Allowing him to leave, only after he has rested, never suggesting betrayal.
She just knows he ain t the same.
And the last time, his drawers were new.
How many thieves got it this good?
How many Queens settle for this too?
Who is the criminal and what is royal to a court jester and a crumb snatcher?
Everyone wanna sit on a throne.
Who's willing to admit that they don't belong there?
Surely not them.
Hell, they fuck on purple satin.

Lauryn Hill Where R U Darlin?

Lauryn Hill where r u darlin?

Cause hardly I'm evolvin without u.

Who knew that your Buffalo Soldier, dred lock'd Rasta
would betray U. Play U as concubine when he
escorted U into Royalty. U bore his legacy. A Marley
Queen. The same loyalty U showed the camp before
it turned into a carnival.

U turned refugee.

U were trampled on but U stammered on, so badgered
on.

No longer miseducated more like catalepsy,
your reality sedated + coked up.

        Yea this is the real ting.

So U numb up U stayed fucked up. No true religion
now but U like Zuleika now, high + pretty in makeup,
wow
And I have heard them say it was the dick that made U
flip, but I know it was these hits of dreams come
true.

Those back shots a part of the scheme for riches
beyond the ghettos of New Jeru.

Cause flipping on those dirty mattresses never suited
U.

Simply put.

It won't what superheroes do.

U were our storm, U were our Wonder Woman.
My eyes haven't left the sky.

Lauryn Hill where R U darlin? I'm not the same without
U.

I thought U had factored in the Xs and found Zion. Now
U, smoking up your baby daddy's stash + crying over
Curtis Mayfield tracks. The lines must lead straight to
your veins. I remember U spat,

–I'm more powerful than 2 Cleopatras†
Never could I have imagined that there would be two
Marc Anthonys.

The same tragedy that brought down Egypt +
Rome, ravaged thru your mind, soul, + home. America
called the feds + U became the casualty.

The war on Lauryn Hill + it saddens me.

'Cause caged birds with clipped wings Don't Sing.

I turn my lights down low and open the window
curtains,

I am certain that the crickets + the moon,
remember U.

I have never forgotten, the Black Janis Joplin.
I've studied your lyrics like doctrines

Every style U rocked, I jocked it.

If they gave me a multiple choice test of the best
female emcee to date, and U won't on it?
I'd write U in as an option!

Stop it!

Baby girl, in retrospect, I never dreamed U'd leave in

summer. Honestly, I still can't believe that you've left at all.

But they sucked U dry of your sweetest things.
And you drowned yourself in the mysteries of your inequities,

+ it all fell down.

Somehow U lost 1, but U still have me.

Come back please.

Because I think it was more of a misdirection than a miseducation.

We all know thru U
what the end of a high means,
+ what it fiends for

Urgh!

Honestly. I'd prefer you not smile when u lied in my
face or to laugh when u disrespect me.
Different levels of acceptances I suppose.
I have children. The majority of the men I've known are
motherfuckers in this respect alone.
Mother lovers are rare n few.
Children lovers as well. But if they were puppies
niggas would really b trying to show off. Treats n
walks n pooper scooping. I laugh at cringes for
changing a diaper, or taking a walk with the child from
these same motherfuckin, not mother loving people.
excuse my candor.
Now about this bitch.
So...I wear her favorite color often or something? The
city on my shirt is just a city on my shirt do u have
an attachment to the city on this shirt cause I can't
really see U making all this hoopla over its colors. I
prefer to wear red or yellow or green or black. U like
me in pink. This shirt is red and black and green with a
city written huge across it. And u really like this shirt.
I can't help but think she must've fucked you good in
that city.
In a conversation about –baby mamas†
Education versus survival verses duty verses promise.
Daily thoughts.
The club, getting some head, clothes or being,
Pretty or skinny or youthful are not.
My bags and my weaves and the shows I watch on tv
paint another picture huh?
Well, u can't beat it. I'll b DAT.

Sex makes it into the realm of daily thought by way of avoidance or need. So sex isn't necessarily sexy. But I still am and most douche bags are. Its a shame...and also how ugly niggas end up getting some pussy.
In conversation about work and craft,
brown nosing irks me. U corny muthafucker.
Female brown nosing as well. Spit the dick out drop the balls.
And for what...now your success got taint on it.
Hate to love me, fuck it. I ll know I made it.
I cried all day. Smoked all day. Ate all day and thought about money.
And I guess the best thought I had today was to not make a call or send a text or answer the phone.
I mean, there is always a way to do it legit too.
Sacrifice ya know?
Satisfied, not so much. Had I not said these things would u know when u saw me next, probably not. I needed today. I need everyday actually. Not people or things or poems or love or money or comfort. I just need to wake up tomorrow, well enough to continue trying.
By my mother loving self.

Hair

She wakes up to hair on the pillowcase. She washes
her hair and it falls out on her shoulders in the suds.
She picks the hair out and it rips and it shreds.
Left scattered on the bathroom sink.
The mind don't control the body.
If it did this wouldn't be her reality.
Everyday she tells herself she isn t sad, that she isn't
tired. She tells herself she is damaged but she will
heal.
Everyday she hears she is strong. Everyday she hears
she is, beautiful.
Everyday she adds ornament to hide battle wound
Everyday she defends armor.
–I am natural!† she screams internally at their glaring
naps, their judging crowns.
Shea Butter scented sneak disses fill her vision.
It's almost as if she can feel each follicle give up, one
by one.
Her shield protects her.
The mane of a lion she prefers.
Its pride suits her.
Makes her feel stronger.
The stress not controlling her appearance.
Her mind knows that they can't see this and she keeps
up her smile.
Absorbs their stares and answers their questions
about black beauty.
She is their Black Beauty.
She is their example.
Her conscious struggles with the guilt of knowing her

body has not healed from being the poor kid, or her
stepfather being sent up the road,
Each hair falls and reminds her of New York, reminds
her of cold water and potatoes, reminds her of May
third
The patches speak of the night he tried to kill her, of
the nights she filled herself with poisons and greed
Unseen to them.
Ornament covers new growth.
Pride adorns her hopefulness
A dresser full of oils and creams to heal a battle
wound that won't scab
U didn't know that
Just talked about her weave

U Think, U Thought, U Knew

U think, U thought, U knew. U stop U know. U thought to think. U stop. U think. You knew or so U thought. What returns to the Earth must once again bloom, that s what I ve been taught. It will. A life avenged by red + silver roses, while vengeance is swallowed whole by birth.

The gift of creation presents revolution. Science meets God. This will all get logical again. He can rest in peace. Although a piece of me fails to believe he ever will. A revolution conceived every day, but he will. We will one day. I think. You thought. That we knew that he was your homeboy, your cousin, your classmate, your brother, your favorite students, your teammate, your lover, your nephew. But he is her son + his name is Mike. Last time it was Kendrick. After that Trayvon + Jordan. Before them it was Eric.

Hoodies up became the proclamation.

Now our bitter faces are waging war on Black Friday we martyrs of melancholy melees + marches.

Whispered to my partner thru the darkness, Baby, there is a war outside.

2014 feels like the 60s!

It seems as if the bloodsuckers never suffer and the mothers are left to endure burning soles, aching calves, broken hearts Found memories.

This Black Girl Lost stands tall.

Holds her son on her hip while two daughters slide their tiny fingers into her belt loops never breaking her stride. The babies bounce off of her backside, casting a maternal shadow. A pale horse, colored in Black indigo. And no she cant say she graduated any college. Left the institution but still pursues the knowledge. Whispers to her partner thru the darkness, Baby there is a war outside.

And Winnie's tribe vibes thru her lips, she gives her Nelson a kiss, spits I gave U loyalty. 26 years I lied flat on my back, stared up at a ceiling + never once asked God why. Silenced shots sweep Soweto's savannahs. Scattered the shepherds. Jar bombs jar moms in Johannesburg. + they run with their children in their arms. They kiss. She spits

police pursuits from Poqouson to Portsmouth. will taze, spray, beat u in the face

from patrol to IA

men running with the faces of children on their arms.

peace not residing in this field.

In these streets.

Baby there is a war outside. But they keep fighting. We keep fighting. U taught us that.

Or has jail made u forget that u are king, even if a cell becomes your throne.

I think. She thought. We know the energy is sucked up in a vacuum of cubicles, warehouses, kitchens, angry bedrooms + nuked dinners. Reposted, stolen + played out like blurred lines

while the inner city remains blue, romanced in Marvins room + casually ingesting mockingbirds eye viewed reflection of disturbia thru the cornea live at 6. all 3 of my eyes blink. you d think, they d think. said the shotgun to the head. the wine bottle by the bed

screaming, Mother Nature is a whore!

I understand that God will never get the respect she deserves. Like at first glance, arent I just another baby mama from the hood? I thought, Insignificant is the science that doesnt teach faith. I mean why wonder when u dont believe? Mother Fucker. I know what different environments produce.
The blacker the flow the slacker my noose.

It's the hiphop in my heart, the forgiveness on my tongue, the sincerity when I speak. The way I put on. Im a woman. Phenomenally. Phenomenal woman that's me. Never judge strength by its measure, the slightest things carry.

They tried to bury us. They didn t know we were seeds said a Mexican proverb that I read on a meme,

savored like a steak dinner. Digested. Licked my fingers + whispered to my partner thru the darkness,

the revolution will come from the gut

You better know it.

Colophon

Cocoa Blues was originally published by BookWook
Press Collective in September 2015.
Editions limited to 30 copies.

Author
Taz Weysweete

Editor
Claire LeDoyen

Cover
Ida Stein, Claire LeDoyen, Lindsay Guim

Design+Typesetting
Lindsay Guim

Reformatting for 2nd & 3rd Edition
J. Scott Wilson, August 2016

Text
News Gothic, News Gothic Bold; a realist sans-serif typeface designed by Morris Fuller Benton, and released by the American Type Founders (ATF) in 1908

www.ingramcontent.com/pod-product-compliance
Lightning Source LLC
LaVergne TN
LVHW051021080826
845145LV00009B/2736

* 9 7 8 1 9 5 2 7 7 3 2 5 9 *